D0423027

HOW AMERICA

LOST HER

A History of the Sexual Revolution

INNOCENCE

Also available by Steve Gallagher
At the Altar of Sexual Idolatry
At the Altar of Sexual Idolatry Workbook
A Biblical Guide to Counseling the Sexual Addict
Create in Me a Pure Heart
Intoxicated With Babylon
Irresistible to God
A Lamp Unto My Feet
Living in Victory
Out of the Depths of Sexual Sin
Pressing on Toward the Heavenly Calling
The Walk of Repentance

These materials may be obtained through:

Pure Life Ministries
14 School Street
Dry Ridge, KY 41035
(888) PURELIFE - to order
(859) 824-4444
(859) 813.0005 - FAX
www.purelifeministries.org

History of the Sexual Revolution
Copyright © 2005 by Steve Gallagher.
All rights reserved. No part of this book may be
reproduced in any form except for brief quotations,
without written permission from the author.

ISBN: 0-9758832-3-2
EAN 978-0-9758832-3-5

*Special thanks to Dr. Judith Reisman
and Colonel & Mrs. Ray.*

"Purity for Life"

*I dedicate this book to Don, Tim, Buddy, Randall,
and all my other friends at the
American Family Association who daily
fight for the decency of our country.*

table of CONTENTS

1 *The Emergence of the Sexual Subculture in America*   9

2 *The Sexual Revolution*   29

3 *The Sex-For-Sale Industry*   47

4 *The Sexploitation of Youth*   73

   Epilogue   85

   Notes   89

CHAPTER ONE

THE EMERGENCE of the Sexual Subculture IN AMERICA

In the long history of the war between good and evil, Satan has used many wicked men and women to further his kingdom of darkness. Voltaire mocked Christianity during the Renaissance. Darwin invented a theory that displaced God as Creator. Lenin launched godless communism. Each of these men left behind a dark legacy that affected the world well beyond their lifetimes.

In post-World War II America, Satan encountered a problem: a strong Judeo-Christian ethic that kept the country locked into a mindset of decency.

Although there were exceptions who lived in lasciviousness, most citizens led respectable lives. This was "The Greatest Generation" that so selflessly sacrificed themselves during the War. Any attempt to overthrow this prevailing uprightness would be no easy undertaking. It would require a very special man. The devil found him in Alfred Kinsey.

Kinsey received a strict, Methodist upbringing in Hoboken, New Jersey. He was a sickly child who felt inferior to other boys. Nevertheless, at age 17, Alfred joined the Boy Scouts, eventually becoming a Scout leader while in college. "His tent, with his 'nature library' (nudist magazines) of a dozen volumes, was a rendezvous for dozens of campers during the day and well into the night, even after taps had sounded and we were supposedly tucked in," wrote a fellow counselor later.[1] Kinsey, a bisexual, apparently abused his position to seduce the boys entrusted into his care.

If there was ever a spiritual struggle going on inside him, it didn't last long. According to Wardell Pomeroy, his closest confidant and associate in later years, Kinsey's crisis with Christianity began when he prayed for a college friend who could not stop masturbating—to no avail. His unbelief grew as he studied the evolutionary teachings of Charles Darwin in college. Eventually he became a devoted atheist, completely throwing off the shackles of Christianity which to him were too restrictive.

Kinsey majored in zoology, with a special interest in gall wasps. While in school he met another student who shared this same interest, Clara Bracken McMillan, whom he married in 1921. He eventually graduated from college and landed a job teaching zoology at Indiana University. However, his interest in animals and insects began to dwindle as he increasingly gave himself over to the true love of his life: sex.

In 1938, he was invited to teach a marriage course at IU. Although marital sexuality had its part in the curriculum—albeit a small one—Alfred de-emphasized the other subjects that were supposed to be covered and used the class as a platform to teach his own distorted perspectives on sex. Students were given extremely intrusive questionnaires regarding the most private and intimate details of their lives. One girl complained that she felt "raped" by the questions. While some faculty members disapproved of the heavy emphasis being placed upon sex, Herman Wells, the school president, impatiently dismissed their concerns. He was openly excited about what was going on and became one of Kinsey's most ardent supporters.

Meanwhile, Kinsey felt inspired to apply to the Rockefeller Foundation for a grant for his "research" in the field of sexology. Surprisingly, this unknown zoologist was granted generous funding. Alfred did not realize that his ideas were exactly what the Council on Foreign Relations—which was heavily influenced if not controlled by the Rockefellers—needed to propagate their own godless agenda. Not only did the Rockefellers fund much of Kinsey's work, but they also used their enormous propaganda department to promote his ideas. However, this would not fully unfold for several years.

In the meantime, Kinsey was on a roll. He was authorized to hire an entire staff to help him in his "research." Every staff member—and wife if the man had one—was expected to provide Kinsey with a complete sexual history. This "confidential" information would later be used to keep wayward souls in line. Eventually, staff members were pressured to participate in homosexuality, wife swapping, and other forms of sexual perversion.

The "uncommitted" were weeded out.

The truth of what went on behind the soundproof walls which he had installed in his "laboratory" would not become fully known for years to come. Not only had the staff become engaged in perversion, but they were also bringing in outside subjects to be observed in the throes of passion. Nothing was taboo or sacred. Every kind of deviancy was displayed—and even filmed—in front of Kinsey's crew.

Like most evil men, Kinsey was a manipulator and an obsessive controller of those around him. Everything that occurred in what became known as the Kinsey Institute was shrouded behind an impenetrable wall of secrecy. The only ones privy to the real story were his staff members: men and women who were implicated by their own complicity and lived under the threat of having their most personal details exposed.

As Kinsey's work gained momentum, the importance of presenting a scholarly image to the public became increasingly clear to him and his staff. This was 1940s America and painstaking care had to be taken to convey their work in the proper light. Alfred, Clara (who had also become involved in the sexual activities taking place) and their two children were presented as a decent, midwestern family. Photographers were forbidden to take unauthorized pictures of Alfred. The only photographs released were carefully staged to present the scholarly persona he wished to convey.

Alfred Kinsey's years of legitimate research on gall wasps provided him the needed confidence to present himself as a bonafide scientist. As a recognized expert in the field of zoology, it was not a huge step to go into another field of study. Indeed, in the Darwinian scheme of things, the study of animals (zoology) and man (anthropology) were closely related. In Darwin's mind, man was just another species of animal. As a mere beast, the craving for sexual satisfaction is simply a normal biological urge. Kinsey built on this Darwinian formula to espouse his belief that sexual urges—of any kind—should not be stymied.

Darwin's teachings—now warmly embraced in American academics—formed the basis for Kinsey's theories. With the full weight of Darwin's evolutionary teachings behind him, he was able to sell his message to the field of academia. Under the guise of scientific research, Kinsey's ideas were widely accepted in scholastic circles. With the support of nearly the entire American collegiate system in his corner, there would be no stopping him.

The Truth Behind Kinsey's Studies

As the eyes of the world turned to the insanity occurring in Europe, Kinsey hired a sizeable staff and engaged in serious, scientific study of human sexuality; or so people were led to believe. He was fascinated with every kind of deviancy known to man and was intensely interested in what went on in the minds of masochists, sadists, child molesters, and so on. He took his sexual history questionnaires—refined over the years since the simplistic one he used with students in his marriage class—into the prisons where he could interview as many sexual offenders as he desired. He also interviewed hundreds of homosexuals, receiving and compiling sexual histories from each.

Dr. Judith Reisman, the woman who first exposed Kinsey's fraud in 1981, explains how skewed the data was that the Kinsey team compiled as the basis for their findings. "Kinsey claimed to document the sexual life of average Americans but the truth was that his 'reliable' male sample was roughly 86 percent aberrant, (prisoners, homosexual activists, pimps, hold-up men, thieves, prostitutes) while his 'average' women were similarly aberrant, including prostitutes redefined as 'married women.' Naturally, Kinsey selected only young, comely, likewise sexually dysfunctional males for his 'science' team, most of whom were his lovers."[2]

In June 1944, as the war raged in the European and Pacific theaters, Kinsey got wind of a pedophile in Arizona named Rex King (given the pseudonym "Mr. Green" in Kinsey's writings) who was journaling in explicit detail his abuse of children. As part of his sexual routine, King recorded everything about his experiences with each child, including using a stopwatch to time the child's reactions to his abuse. Kinsey, obsessed with such information, was ecstatic over this news. He immediately headed west, meeting King out in the desert where he had buried his journals. The exchange was made and Kinsey took his "treasure" back to Indiana.

Over the next three years, Kinsey compiled other "data" and completed his groundbreaking book *Sexual Behavior in the Human Male*. The now infamous chapter five—dealing with adult-child sex—was almost entirely based upon King's experiences. Kinsey presented this "data" so clinically that no one ever guessed it was actually a part of the sick behavior of a demented child molester.

One of his most revolutionary "findings"—that children were sexual beings from birth—was based on such skewed data. "We have a whole chapter in which children have been tortured for this so-called scientific data," says Dr. Reisman. "This data suggests that a minimum of 317, and a maximum of 1,200 children (were abused), with some boys being sexually raped around the clock."

Evidence seems to indicate that Mr. King was abusing children until 1954, more than 10 years after meeting Kinsey. "If Green was sexually abusing children until 1954—and Kinsey's last book came out in 1953—that would certainly mean that all the violence and all the abuse was going on throughout the entire time Kinsey was collecting this data," Reisman says. "Based on Kinsey's writings, he approved fully of adult-child sexual interactions," she continues. "Not only that, he recommended that adults could effectively aid their children to have better sexual lives by giving them 'orgasms' at a very early age."

The story really gets gruesome when one reads between the lines of some of Kinsey's accounts of child abuse. Reisman states, "Kinsey recruited pedophiles and incestuous males and females to sexually abuse up to 2,035 fainting, screaming and struggling children, as young as two months of age, for his so-called child sex 'data.'" This was explained away with scientific jargon under the premise that children want to have sex but need time to get used to it. One can only imagine the horror some of these children experienced under the approving smile of Alfred Kinsey. According to insider/biographer James Jones, he was "a closeted and violent sado-masochistic, adulterous, bi-homosexual, pornography producer/addict and a bully."

This is the man to whom American academics looked to provide "scientific research" in the area of sexual function. His "studies" established the direction in the field of human sexuality for several decades. Virtually every study done in this field stems directly or indirectly from his findings. If Kinsey was exceptional at anything in life, it was his ability to present ridiculous and even dangerous information as scientific fact. Unquestionably, he was one of the supreme imposters of the 20th Century.

The Overthrow of Common Law

During the time of Kinsey's research, heterosexual intercourse within the confines of a traditional marriage was the only lawful way to engage in sex. Within the various state and federal penal codes, there were 52 sexual acts that were outlawed, ranging from adultery to rape. Kinsey was determined to have most of these laws overturned and expunged from the books. The remaining statutes—those he knew the American public would insist upon retaining—he would seek to weaken in every possible way.

One of Kinsey's main contentions was that sexual deviancy was not abnormal but actually the norm for 95% of the population. This supposition was based on the enormously skewed data he accumulated—not from typical Americans—but from pedophiles, rapists, homosexuals, and others involved in sexual perversion. As one of his supporters within the legal system gushed, "One of the conclusions of the Kinsey Report…the sex offender is not a monster…but an individual who is not very different from others in his social group…"[3]

Another falsehood he presented as scientific fact was that children are sexual and potentially orgasmic from birth (womb to tomb). This hypothesis undercut every law aimed at protecting children from sexual predators. If his contentions were true, then child molesters were actually doing their victims a favor. Dr. Reisman comments on the ramifications of Kinsey's findings:

> Forces within the therapeutic field fostered sympathy for the perpetrator and 'treatment' supplanted common law penalties. *Sexual Behavior in the Human Female* (1953) added to the mix the stunning finding that no real harm from rape or molestation were found in the 4,441 female interviews that comprised the second Kinsey Report. If no measurable harm from rape and molestation occurred in the lives of "normal" American women, then the penalties for such crimes were unwarranted. The Kinsey

Reports went further and claimed that half of American women in the 1940s and 50s are not virgins when they married.[4]

As Kinsey's influence grew, others began to catch the "vision" of a more liberal society with looser morals. Some proponents wrote books that supported his arguments, giving him even greater credibility. As his work gained momentum, a small radical element within the American Bar Association decided to use his "findings" to overhaul the Penal Code, especially those laws pertaining to sexual offenses.

These lawyers decided that—in light of this new scientific knowledge—the current structure of law was anachronistic and in need of revision. It was then that the ABA produced the "Model Penal Code" (MPC). Rather than the general public or their elected representatives deciding what was acceptable behavior, this small group of elites took matters into their own hands with the aid of "scientific experts." As one of them boasted in 1955, "we mean to act as if we were a legislative commission, charged with construction of an ideal penal code."[5]

The MPC immediately set out to transform laws regarding sexual activity from being morality-based to being "scientifically-based." Consensual sexual relations with adults should be legalized. Moreover, this new legal perspective paved the way to abolish laws against adultery, homosexuality and a myriad of other illicit activities.

Perhaps even more serious was the undercutting of victims' rights. The Kinsey perspective of children being sexual beings had a great influence upon molestation laws. As one adherent wrote, "...hysteria surrounding these events (abuse) usually did more harm than the events themselves, which sometimes gave pleasure."[6] Although Kinsey and the liberal jurists who embraced his views would have been happy to expunge all the laws against molestation, they knew the American public would never stand for it. Nevertheless, Kinsey's suppositions lessened the perceived seriousness of it.

This same mentality extended itself to rape victims as well. Kinsey's perspective that "women want it, no matter how much they might say they don't" had a similar effect upon laws against rape. Prior to Kinsey, a preponderance of evidential weight was given to the victim's testimony, but after the changes were enacted, it became his word against hers. Furthermore, there had to be proof that there was "physical force sufficient to overcome earnest resistance."[7]

Armed with Kinsey's perverted perspectives on sexuality, the MPC threw out or weakened nearly every single law relating to sexual crimes.

The Hidden Agenda Behind Sex Education

Kinsey's influence reached into one more important sector of society: academia. In 1964, Dr. Mary Calderone, former medical director of Planned Parenthood, began the Sex Information and Educational Council of the United States (SIECUS) as an educational arm of the Kinsey Institute.

Calderone's objective from the outset was to open the minds of children to Kinsey's concepts about sexuality. She shared his view that America was too intolerant of homosexuality, promiscuity and even child molestation. With the (undue) credibility and vast resources of the Kinsey Institute behind her (as well as sizable donations from the Playboy Foundation), she openly campaigned to establish a curriculum of sex(*uality*) education for America's young people. Calderone, like the liberal lawyers of MPC before her, persuaded academics that only the experts should be in a position to make decisions regarding sexuality. "Sexuality education should only be taught by specially trained teachers. Professionals responsible for sexuality education must receive specialized training in human sexuality, including the philosophy and methodology of sexuality education."[8]

When her efforts were rightly attacked by pro-family organizations, Calderone learned to evade criticism by masking the real objectives of her organization. To get at the real agenda of SIECUS, one must look deeper than the carefully prepared statements made for the benefit of the press. For instance, one of their primary objectives is the open acceptance and legalization of pedophilia. If this seems like an exaggerated interpretation of their agenda, consider the following statements by those directly involved with SIECUS and the Kinsey Institute:

> "Providing today's society with a very
> deep awareness of the vital importance

of infant and childhood sexuality' is now the primary goal of SIECUS."—Mary Calderone[9]

"What do we know about situations in which young children and older people, stronger people, have had a sexual relationship of one kind or another that has been pleasant, and the child feels good about it because it's warm and seductive and tender?" Mary Calderone[10]

"...the idea of childhood sexuality...has forever affected our conception of human sexual development and thoughts about sex education."—Wardell Pomeroy[11]

"...incest between adults and younger children can also prove to be a satisfying and enriching experience. Incestuous relationships can—and do—work out well."—Wardell Pomeroy[12]

"This is a peculiarly American problem—the withdrawal of all touching contact—and children, especially girls, feel the lack very keenly…How many adolescent girls have not said, 'It's the only time I feel someone really loves me.'? Who knows how much psychic damage we cause our children with such well-meant yet inhuman attitudes? Surely the time has come when we can and should deal with the incest taboo by finding out the facts, all of them, and acting rationally and sensibly about them, whatever they may be."—James Rainey, EdD[13]

"The fact that few investigators have examined the sexuality of people early in the life span has been attributed by John Money to the taboos that surround childhood eroticism."—Elizabeth Allgeier[14]

Notably, these statements were made while in the friendly confines of others who shared their views.

On April 14, 1980, *Time Magazine* ran an article entitled, *Attacking the Last Taboo*. The author saw right through the SIECUS hypocrisy when he wrote:

The SIECUS Report...published a major article attacking the incest taboo. Though the journal's editor, Mary Calderone, and her colleagues ran an ingenuous editorial denying that the article was advocating anything, the piece in fact depicted the taboo as mindless prejudice. Wrote the author, James W. Rainey: "We are roughly in the same position today regarding incest as we were a hundred years ago with respect to our fears of masturbation..."

But most of the pro-incest thought rises logically enough from the premises of the sex-research establishment: all forms of consensual sexuality are good, or at least neutral; problems arise not from sex, but from guilt, fear and repression. That kind of faith is bound to lead its believers in crusades against all sexual prohibitions, including incest.

Now, nearly fifty years since Kinsey's death, the evil movement he spawned in a midwestern university is still unfolding throughout Western Civilization. Kinsey has rightly been labeled the father of the sexual revolution. What he began has accounted for millions of corrupted lives, destroyed families, out-of-wedlock pregnancies, and their subsequent abortions. Countless women have been raped and children molested as a direct result of what Satan unleashed through the efforts of this monster. Surely Kinsey's heritage can be summed up with the words expressed about his master: "The thief comes only to steal, and kill, and destroy…"

THE SEXUAL Revolution

If Alfred Kinsey legitimized illicit sex to the academic world, Hugh Hefner made it popular to the public. In a day when moral decency was greatly respected, Hefner glamorized the idolization of the woman's body and a promiscuous lifestyle. His carefree approach to life made him the perfect man to launch *Playboy* magazine.

Hefner, like Kinsey before him, rejected his strict Methodist upbringing. From early on, he desired a life unrestrained by the shackles of morality. In high school, he spent his free time cartooning and daydreaming about sex. He even wrote an essay once criticizing the repression of sexuality in society—an ominous prelude to his eventual life's work.

Hefner was attending the University of Illinois in 1948 when Kinsey's book, *Sexual Behavior in the Human Male*, was released. The excited 21-year-old praised it in the college newspaper. "It was a revelation for me," Hefner later stated, "because it confirmed the hypocrisy for me, the gap between what we said and what we actually did." Of course, Kinsey's conjectures were all based on lies, but his writings told Hefner what he wanted to hear.

He eventually became the editor of a satirical magazine, *Shaft*, in which he introduced a feature entitled, "Coed of the Month." With an I.Q. of 156, he finished college in 2½ years and went to work for *Esquire* magazine. Around this time, Hefner also married his high school sweetheart, Millie Williams, whom he eventually divorced 10 years later. Their only child, Christie, now oversees the Playboy Empire.

Young Hefner, feeling restricted and unfulfilled, eventually left *Esquire* and set out to design his own magazine. In 1953, he acquired some nude photos of Marilyn Monroe, taken years before when she was still known as Norma Jean. Armed with this treasure, Hefner borrowed every dime he could lay his hands on and launched *Playboy* magazine. To his surprise, that first edition sold 50,000 copies. Although it was illegal to mail obscene material, for some reason the U. S. Postal Service never brought charges against Hefner.

"It was never my intention to be a revolutionary," he gushed recently. "My intention was to try to create a mainstream men's magazine that included sex in it. That turned out to be a very revolutionary idea. That's because we lived in what I then and now viewed as a very repressive, sick society."

Playboy was a hit—especially amongst the college crowd. Hefner used the windfall from his inaugural issue to fund subsequent issues. He never dreamed of the success that would follow. In June of 1963, he was arrested in Chicago on obscenity charges for a pictorial entitled, *The Nudist Jayne Mansfield*, but he was eventually acquitted. Now nothing could stand in his way.

The 1960s were a boon for *Playboy*. "Suddenly, the morality of our nation took a major nosedive as public prayer was banned in the nation's schools, social and political unrest became more pronounced, and the debacle called The Vietnam War got underway. By the end of the decade, drug abuse was rampant, sexual promiscuity was the norm, and anti-government riots were taking place across the land." [15] *Playboy* rode the crest of this tidal wave of immorality straight through America's most tumultuous decade.

By the time that it went public in 1971, Playboy Enterprises was flying high. Hefner had opened 23 Playboy clubs across the country and was selling seven million magazines a month. But, suddenly, the nation's first successful "girlie" magazine was faced with its greatest threat. However, it didn't come through anti-obscenity laws, or from radical feminists claiming exploitation of women. The danger was that of becoming obsolete, for it was in the early '70s that *Penthouse* and *Hustler* magazines were launched—along with a host of others, all of which featured explicit nudity and sexual content. Hefner, wishing to retain some semblance of dignity, refused to go "all the way" like his competitors. Apparently he knew his giving in would lock him in a race to publish the sleaziest men's magazine on the market. Consequently, *Playboy* remained on the fringes of respectability. The other "rags" could appeal to those looking for the raciest pictures. Hefner determined to maintain *Playboy's* status as a classy "girlie" magazine.

Hefner's Heritage

In a day before the advent of the bikini, Hugh Hefner did the unimaginable—he successfully marketed to the public a magazine featuring nudity. However, his target market wasn't mainstream America as much as it was young men. Dr. Judith Reisman writes, "The magazine's revolution and objective was to get American boys and men to reject their parents' morality and accept *Playboy's* morality as their own."[16] Hefner's success in this endeavor was enormous.

In 1989, he boasted, "*Playboy* freed a generation from guilt about sex, changed some laws and helped launch a revolution or two...*Playboy* is the magazine that changed America."[17] What he says is partially true; his publication certainly affected an entire generation of young men. However, it wasn't so much a release from their feelings of guilt about illicit sex as it was an altering of their perspectives. Young men who, for the most part, held to the conviction "no sex without love" became terribly contaminated by this new brand of carefree promiscuity.

Without question, Hefner opened the door for easy access to pornography in the United States. Amazingly, he did it alone for nearly 20 years. By the time *Penthouse* and *Hustler* came on the scene, *Playboy* had already won the initial battle for indecency and overcome the stigma of nudity. With that line crossed, nothing would stop the great outpouring of pure filth that eventually followed.

The scope of Hefner's influence on American society, though, extended beyond his pioneering the first successful girlie magazine. Not only did he affect people's perception of nudity, he also popularized a lifestyle that was previously unknown. "Suddenly bachelorhood was a choice, one decorated with intelligent drinks, hi-fis and an urbane apartment that put white picket fences to shame," coos one admirer. "Sophistication had become a viable option for men: The Playboy universe encouraged appreciation of 'the finer things'— literature, a good pipe, a cashmere pullover, a beautiful lady. America was seeing the advent of the urban single male who, lest his subversive departure from domestic norms suggest homosexuality, was now enjoying new photos of nude women every month." [18]

As his purveyance of smut expanded, Hefner began to flex his financial and editorial muscles. In 1965, he instituted the Playboy Foundation as a means to funnel funds into pet causes—to date, at least $11 million. Mary Calderone and SIECUS were among the first beneficiaries of this "philanthropy."

Presently Hefner uses both his money and his immensely popular magazine to further his underlying agenda. As Reisman charges, "What non-consumers do not know (and many *Playboy* consumers overlook) is that *Playboy* has always been much more than a 'girlie' or 'men's magazine.' It has long been a bully pulpit for a world view that judges men according to their tally of sexual conquests."[19]

Now at age 76, Hugh Hefner undoubtedly reflects on the past 50 years with a sense of true accomplishment. He has likely been sexually involved with thousands of women and spent millions frolicking around the globe. His magazine is among the most successful periodicals of all time.

Indeed, he has contributed greatly to America's present state of moral decay and desensitization. But soon he will die and stand before his Maker.

The Emergence of the Gay Rights Movement

As the heterosexual community experimented with their newfound sexual freedoms, a new group emerged to challenge America's already weakening morality. Homosexuals saw the winds of change blowing through the U.S. in the '60s as an opportunity to push for their own rights and freedoms. They were fed up with what they considered prejudice toward their chosen lifestyle. Needless to say, the turmoil simmering across the nation was about to boil over into the gay community.

On June 27th, 1969, eight police officers entered the Stonewall Inn located in Greenwich Village, New York—an unlicensed tavern allegedly run by the Mob. To the police, this was just another raid on a gay bar, and at first, everything went according to plan. The bartender, failing to produce a copy of a valid liquor license, was ushered along with a number of his customers out to the waiting "paddy-wagon."

What transpired next has been the subject of some debate. Some say that a "butch" lesbian resisted arrest. Others say a "drag queen" started screaming at the officers. Regardless of what sparked the incident, it erupted within moments into a full-scale riot. The mob, angered over what appeared to be nothing more than a "police shakedown," began throwing coins and then bottles at the beleaguered policemen. "They were throwing more than lace hankies," one detective quipped. "I was almost decapitated by a slab of thick glass. It was thrown like a discus and just missed my throat by inches. The beer can didn't miss, though, it hit me right above the temple."

A few days later, in an article written for *The New York Daily News*, "Homo Nest Raided; Queen Bees Are Stinging Mad," reporter Jerry Lisker described the incident:

> All hell broke loose when the police entered the Stonewall...A crowd had formed in front of the Stonewall and the customers were greeted with cheers of encouragement from the gallery.
>
> The whole proceeding took on the

aura of a homosexual Academy Awards Night. The Queens pranced out to the street blowing kisses and waving to the crowd. A beauty of a specimen named Stella wailed uncontrollably while being led to the sidewalk in front of the Stonewall by a cop...

The crowd began to get out of hand, eye witnesses said. Then, without warning, Queen Power exploded with all the fury of a gay atomic bomb. Queens, princesses and ladies-in-waiting began hurling anything they could get their polished, manicured fingernails on. Bobby pins, compacts, curlers, lipstick tubes and other femme fatale missiles were flying in the direction of the cops. The war was on. The lilies of the valley had become carnivorous jungle plants.

Urged on by cries of "C'mon girls, let's go get 'em," the defenders of Stonewall launched an attack. The cops called for assistance. To the rescue came the Tactical Patrol Force...Official reports listed four injured policemen with 13 arrests. The

War of the Roses lasted about 2 hours
from about midnight to 2 a.m. There was
a return bout Wednesday night.

While the Stonewall Inn riot is considered by
many to be the birth of the "Gay Rights Movement,"
it actually began much earlier.

Homosexuality was practically unheard of
during the first hundred years of our nation. As
the Industrial Age progressed, the growth of urban
centers in the early 1900s attracted small clusters of
homosexuals who began congregating in inner-city
clubs and bars. By the time the '20s came roaring
onto the scene, a "same-sex" subculture had already
sprung up in places like Greenwich Village, San
Francisco's Barbary Coast, and the French Quarter
of New Orleans.

While Americans in the late '40s and early
'50s recovered from the horrors of World War
II, homosexuals quietly mobilized in cities
across the country. Tolerance for this growing
movement was scant during the McCarthy era.
Vice squads routinely raided gay bars and clubs.
In 1953, President Dwight D. Eisenhower issued
an executive order barring homosexuals from

holding federal jobs. Most states had long since adopted sodomy laws.

In November of 1950, a small group of men headed by avowed communist Harry Hay, met together in Los Angeles. They became known as the Mattachine Society; their name derived from a secret anti-establishment group which existed during the Middle Ages. Clusters of these intolerants quietly sprouted up in various cities nationwide. Though short-lived, the Mattachine Society was the beginning of what would become known as the "Homophile Movement."

During the '60s, America experienced a new level of widespread upheaval. Groups such as The Black Panthers sought to drown out the voice of non-violence from civil rights leaders like Dr. Martin Luther King. Feminist organizations, led by militant lesbians, became more vocal in their demands for "women's rights." Anti-war riots broke out across the country. Drug abuse was rampant especially among young people.

This was the volatile environment which ignited the Stonewall riot in 1969. The following year, 5,000 gays and lesbians marched in New York City to commemorate its first anniversary. By 1973, there were nearly 800 gay and lesbian organizations in the U.S. alone. That same year, the American Psychiatric Association (armed with Kinsey's fraudulent report) dropped homosexuality from its list of mental disorders. Within five years, 20 states had repealed their sodomy laws, some going so far as to pass civil-rights protection for homosexuals.

In spite of these political victories, it seemed for a time as though the gay liberation movement would destroy itself through bickering and in-fighting amongst its leaders. An interesting and unanticipated rift developed between gays and lesbians. The Feminist Movement—dominated by lesbians—found itself in an uneasy alliance with the newly emerging "Christian Right." Their mutual stand against the exploitation of women in pornography was not well-received by the large percentage of gay men viewing pornography regularly.

It seemed as though all was lost in 1980 when Ronald Reagan gained the presidency by a landslide victory over Jimmy Carter. The newly-created political conservatism was certain to be a real setback to the gay rights movement. Christian activists such as Anita Bryant, Don Wildmon, and Jerry Falwell successfully organized coalitions of conservatives,

Catholics, fundamentalists, and evangelicals to battle the evils of pornography, abortion, and the homosexual agenda.

Despite this opposition, homosexuality continued to gain acceptance among a growing segment of the American public. Large numbers of men were enticed into same-sex liaisons by the allure of "easy sex." Flagrant perversion and unreserved indulgence marked the new mentality of the '80s, as bathhouses, adult bookstores, and gay nightclubs flourished. Just as the "Sodom-and-Gomorrah" party began to roll forward, a mysterious disease arrived from the shores of Africa: AIDS.

This horrible disease had devastating effects upon the male homosexual community. The freewheeling days of casual sex abruptly ended. The media published pictures of men withering away in the throes of the dreaded plague.

Inexplicably however, the AIDS epidemic breathed new life into gay activism. Quarreling groups reconciled and a newfound compassion for "the cause" welled up from the American public. Most importantly, thousands of previously disinterested homosexuals now became outspoken advocates. Several famous actors and actresses also adopted the new *cause celebre*. The effects were instant and dramatic. For instance, in 1987 over 600,000 people marched in a gay-pride parade in Washington D.C. This momentum continued, culminating in 1993 as over a million participants descended on the streets of the capitol.

The Legalization of Abortion

Amidst the tumultuous backdrop of the '60s and '70s, another storm was about to erupt. A seemingly insignificant event in 1969 would later prove to be a major turning point for the forces of immorality.

Norma McCorvey, 21-years-old and pregnant for the third time, approached prominent Dallas attorney Sarah Weddington about having an abortion, claiming she had been raped. Weddington decided to seize upon this case as an opportunity to contest the criminal abortion laws in Texas which forbade abortion except when the mother's life was in danger. With McCorvey (a.k.a. Jane Roe) as her client, Weddington challenged the constitutionality of these laws. Texas Attorney General, Henry

Wade, mounted a successful defense and the case was rejected.

Undaunted, Weddington filed an appeal four years later with the U.S. Supreme Court, arguing that the abortion laws infringed upon a woman's constitutional rights to privacy. In a controversial decision, the Court agreed and created the "trimester system," based on each three-month period of the pregnancy. During the first trimester, the woman was given the absolute right to have an abortion; during the second, some government regulations were allowed; and during the third, states could restrict or ban abortion (if they chose) unless the woman's life was in jeopardy.

Norma McCorvey later became a born-again Christian and renounced her part in the entire process. "All I did was lie about how I got pregnant. I was having an affair…I did not go to the Supreme Court on behalf of a class of women…I went to Sarah Weddington asking her if she knew how I could obtain an abortion. She and Linda Coffey said they didn't know where to get one. They lied to me just like I lied to them. Sarah already had an abortion. She knew where to get one. Sarah and Linda were just looking for somebody, anybody, to further their own agenda. I was their willing dupe. For this, I will forever be ashamed."[20]

Three decades later, nearly 40 million babies have been put to death in the United States alone—an entire generation annihilated. Perhaps no one feels the enormity of this quite like Norma McCorvey. One day, while at a playground, she noticed there were no children on the swings. "They were swinging back and forth but they were all empty," she told ABC's World News Tonight. "And I just totally lost it, and I thought 'Oh my God. They are empty because there's no children, because they've all been aborted!'"[21]

In the 1960s, proponents of the Sexual Revolution offered to emancipate the American public from its old-fashioned values. The visible results, of course, were bondage, misery and even death. And still, astounding as it may have seemed at the time, a greater tragedy lay ahead. The United States had not yet seen the final consequences of the Pandora's Box opened decades before by one Alfred Kinsey.

CHAPTER THREE

THE Sex-For-Sale INDUSTRY

Social upheaval continued to plague the United States as it entered the 1970s. U.S. soldiers were still fully embroiled in the quagmire of the Vietnam War. Questions about a botched burglary of the Democratic headquarters in Washington, D.C. began to surface. Drug abuse continued to soar among young people. And two brothers from the Columbo Mafia organization named Joseph and Louis Peraino produced an X-rated comedy they hoped would earn them a few thousand dollars in quick profit. D_____ T_____ was filmed mostly in a motel on Biscayne Blvd. in North Miami. It only cost $25,000 to produce, but to the gangsters' amazement, it brought in a staggering $50 million in profit as thousands of Americans flocked into theaters to watch it.

Nobody could have guessed what the long-term ramifications of this movie would be. Other mobsters were quick to get in on the action and soon there was a rash of X-rated movies produced and distributed throughout the country.

The subsequent success of the adult entertainment industry is directly attributable to the social barriers that had been broken down through *Playboy* magazine. The American public had long since been prepared for a further step into the cesspool of immorality.

Even though D_____ T_____ temporarily opened the door for average Americans to openly view pornography, smut quickly receded back into the underground of "closet" behavior. The American public was willing to allow its existence; it just wasn't yet prepared to openly embrace it. Phrases such as, "To each his own," expressed the popular sentiment that people should be allowed to do as they wished—so long as it didn't affect others.

Most people considered pornography viewing to be harmless fun.

Although millions of men became enthralled with X-rated films, viewing them was still considered socially taboo. In other words, a man might go watch one of these movies by himself, but he typically wouldn't tell his friends about it. Thus, a double standard was birthed surrounding the pornography industry. Mafia associates were making hundreds of millions of dollars because men were watching these movies. Pornography had become America's dirty little secret.

At the same time feature films were becoming popular, adult bookstores were popping up by the thousands across the country. Thousands—if not millions—of men were becoming heavily addicted to hardcore pornography. Most sexual addicts preferred the bookstores because they offered private booths that played short 8-millimeter films of people having sex. A man could go into one of these booths and masturbate in private while watching pornography. When he was done, he would simply get in his car and drive away. He didn't have to worry about hiding embarrassing magazines from friends and loved ones.

It wasn't long before homosexuals saw the opportunities to engage in sex with otherwise heterosexual men. As the "straight" male went from booth to booth in his lust-filled condition, homosexuals would make themselves available to satisfy him. Thus, millions of "average Joes" would become involved in homosexual encounters that would have seemed unthinkable to them before being so influenced by the seedy world of pornography.

As the United States moved into the 1980s, a simple technological invention would further entrench pornography into the American culture. When video recorders/players came on the scene, smut producers were quick to see the potential windfall and began producing adult movies by the thousands. Men no longer had to sneak into sleazy adult theaters to watch these full-length films: now they could purchase them and have their own porn library at home.

The adult entertainment industry exploded. Now the trade had its own class of directors, producers, film crews—and, of course, stars and starlets. By the mid-'80s, most of the porn industry had moved to Southern California. According to testimony before the Meese Commission by Captain James Doherty of the L.A.P.D., almost 90% of adult films were produced in Los Angeles. Chief Daryl Gates went on to say that at least 85% of the porn industry was controlled by organized crime.[22]

The "Art" of Striptease Revived

With the emergence of the adult entertainment industry came the desire to see live women in the raw. In the '80s, strip clubs ranging from sleazy, back-alley dives to elegant "gentlemen's" clubs opened across the country.

Burlesque began in the middle of the nineteenth century when comedians in cheap theaters spoofed (or "burlesqued") the operas, plays and social habits of the upper classes. Over time, it became increasingly reliant on the display of shapely, underdressed girls to keep audiences interested. In a time when women went to great lengths to hide their physical form behind frilly dresses, young ladies appearing onstage in revealing costumes became an immediate sensation.

In 1929, striptease entered a new plateau

when a fifteen-year-old girl named Rose Louise Hovick—later known as Gypsy Rose Lee—began her career as a stripper. She brought a new credibility to stripping by her lewd flirtatious patter and seductive costuming. Every era had its star performers. Blaze Starr utilized satin and feathers to enhance her performances in the 1950s. Carol Doda simply used massive injections of silicone to tantalize men in the '60s. By the 1980s, subtle seductiveness had given way to crass nudity.

Striptease—like the rest of the sex-for-sale industry—boomed in the '80s and '90s. According to one source, there are currently 5,700 strip clubs in the U.S., employing approximately 200,000 girls.[23] It seems that the proliferation of pornography has created an enormous army of sexual addicts, every one of whom continually seeks new ways to satisfy his cravings. The strip club has provided one more avenue of illicit activity for the lust-filled man.

The Proliferation of Prostitution

While many men were content watching movies and strippers, others left the adult bookstores and strip clubs in a sexual frenzy looking for opportunities to act out the scenes they had just witnessed. While prostitution has been around since man's earliest days, the explosion of pornography greatly increased the demand for sex-for-hire.

However, there was one more important factor in the tremendous escalation of prostitution in the 1980s and 1990s: drug abuse. It didn't take female drug addicts long to realize that the quickest way to make money was through the immoral use of their bodies. David Sherman, who managed strip clubs for 14 years, testified before the Michigan House Committee on Ethics and Constitutional Law that most of the girls he managed were addicted to drugs. Either they went into stripping to support an existing habit or they began using drugs to deal with the mounting shame of what they were doing. Sherman explained how this worked to his benefit:

> Right from the start, drug and alcohol use is rampant. The dancers call it partying. They don't realize that they are medicating themselves in order to do the work they do...Soon the new dancer starts running around with the more hardened and

seasoned girls, who realize how much easier
their job is being drunk, high or, more often
than not, both. By now she's working until
2 a. m., staying out all night partying after
work, and then grabbing breakfast with
the girls…

Once dancing they get used to being
objectified. It becomes as important to
them to hear how beautiful they are 200
times a day as it is to actually make the
money from the dancing.

Between the use of drugs to medicate
what they do and hearing how beautiful they
are all the time, they soon experience what
I call BDA—Basic Dancer Attitude. This
is when the dancer thinks that no matter
what friends, children, husband and families
think about her, it doesn't matter.

They can all be replaced because all of
the patrons around her find her attractive,
beautiful and idolized. Now, the dancers
are truly caught in the adult scene. With
friends and family gone from their lives,
they exist alone in this dark subculture of
sex, drugs, alcohol and prostitution. All of

Pure Life Ministries

LEADING MEN INTO PURITY SINCE 1986

Since 1986, Pure Life Ministries has been helping Christians
overcome the devastating effects of sexual sin. During that
time, Steve Gallagher and his staff have
passionately labored to bring healing
to this cancer in the Body of Christ.
By consistently emphasizing
repentance, the infallibility of
Scripture and the power of the Holy
Spirit, they are leading a generation
of Christians back to the type of life-
transformation that typified the New
Testament Church.

"Purity for Life"

www.purelifeministries.org

888.PURELIFE

"Everyday I hear from those whose lives are in bondage to pornography. Pure Life offers a much needed ministry to those seeking deliverance from this bondage."

DON WILDMON, American Family Association

"I appreciate your willingness to share your personal experiences with our viewers. I'm sure that many of them were touched and encouraged to hear what God has done in your life."

PAT ROBERTSON, The 700 Club

"Steve, I appreciate your ministry and your work to help people come out of sexual bondage."

DR. D. JAMES KENNEDY, Coral Ridge Ministries

"Thank God for a man like Steve Gallagher, who will tell the truth and let the truth make us free."

The late **DR. EDWIN LOUIS COLE**, Christian Men's Network

"Steve, you have a marvelous ministry and one I really commend you for."

BEVERLY LAHAYE, Concerned Women for America

"I believe you will find in Steve a man of integrity and a person of great desire to forward the work of God."

PASTOR GLEN COLE, The Assemblies of God

"Very few organizations are able to have a success rate when it comes to addiction. Pure Life Ministries is an exception."

JOHN D. DEBRINE - Host, Songtime USA

"I strongly endorse the ministry of Pure Life Ministries and specifically Mr. Steve Gallagher. I commend Steve's ministry, but most of all I commend Steve as a man with spiritual integrity."

DAVID E. MARTIN, CBN University

Pure Life Ministries
MILESTONES

APRIL 1986	*Pure Life Ministries* founded as a support group in Sacramento.
JUNE 1986	*700 Club* films Steve & Kathy Gallagher's testimony.
DECEMBER 1986	Steve Gallagher authors *At the Altar of Sexual Idolatry*.
JANUARY 1988	Steve Gallagher appears on the *Oprah Winfrey Show*.
JANUARY 1989	PLM relocates to Kentucky.
JANUARY 1990	The *Live-In Program* is launched with 6 residents.
MAY 1991	Steve Gallagher appears on *Focus on the Family*.
AUGUST 1991	The *Overcomers-At-Home Program* begins.
DECEMBER 1991	PLM purchases current facility.
JUNE 1992	*48 Hours* films a piece about PLM.
AUGUST 1998	Kathy Gallagher authors *When His Secret Sin Breaks Your Heart*.
MAY 2001	First *Men of Purity* conference presented.
OCTOBER 2003	PLM purchases office building in Dry Ridge, KY.
JANUARY 2005	Steve Gallagher's books begin to be published in Brazil.
JULY 2007	Steve & Kathy Gallagher co-author *Create in Me A Pure Heart: Answers for Struggling Women*.

"Purity for Life"

www.purelifeministries.org

888.PURELIFE

Live-in Program

The Pure Life Ministries Live-In Program is the premier residential program for Christian men seeking God's answers to sexual sin. What began in 1990 with six men has grown into a 55-bed facility on 45 acres in Kentucky. The goal of this 6-month program is not just the breaking of the power of outward sin, but the complete transformation of a man's heart. To date, hundreds of men have experienced such a transformation.

KEY Features TO SUCCESS:

- *The presence of God that brings a man into deep repentance*
- *Separation from the old sources of temptation*
- *Development of a life of discipline*
- *Biblical counseling by men who have overcome sexual sin themselves*

Overcomers At-Home Program

The Overcomers At-Home Program (OCAH) is especially beneficial for those whose current situation does not demand a residential program. The OCAH program is also available for wives and women struggling with sexual sin. The curriculum of this 12-week program is exclusively designed to bring each counselee to true repentance and teach him or her how to live in daily victory over sin.

KEY Features TO SUCCESS:

- *The same teaching materials used in the Live-In Program*
- *12 weekly counseling sessions over the phone*
- *Trained biblical counselors who know how to instill hope as they disciple participants into freedom*
- *Counseling for wives experiencing the devastating effects of their husband's sin*

Counseling Helpline

When secret sin is exposed, it usually brings with it the need for sound, biblical decisions. In 2005, PLM began to meet this growing need by making their wealth of expertise available to those in crisis by creating a counseling helpline. Since most Helpline callers are facing a critical life decision, this service assists them in choosing the right course of action.

THE PLM Counseling STAFF

All of Pure Life Ministries' counselors are trained and certified in biblical counseling through the International Association of Biblical Counselors. Having graduated the Live-In Program, each male counselor knows what it takes to find victory over sexual sin. Likewise, female counselors have passed through the suffering and shame of their husband's sin.

Pure Life Ministries
SPEAKINGMINISTRY

Living in sexual purity is one of the toughest battles Christian men face in today's sexualized culture. And, as demand for effective answers to sexual sin increases, the *Pure Life Ministries* speaking ministry continues to expand and adapt.

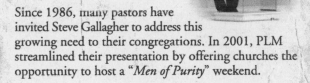

Since 1986, many pastors have invited Steve Gallagher to address this growing need to their congregations. In 2001, PLM streamlined their presentation by offering churches the opportunity to host a *"Men of Purity"* weekend.

Since that time, Steve Gallagher and his team have ministered to many men's groups throughout North and South America. They are prepared to address a number of issues in various settings:

- Men's conferences on purity
- Teaching seminars for pastors and counselors
- High school and college groups
- Seminars for women, wives and couples

"Purity for Life"

www.purelifeministries.org

888.PURELIFE

this perverse living, to the dancer, is now just part of her normal lifestyle.

After a couple of years at this level, the dancer realizes she is getting older and attempts to fit back into society. She tries boyfriends, school or really anything to cling to what is normal. Realizing that she cannot live in both worlds, she returns to the subculture of the adult business, actually despising the real world. This leads to more dependency on drugs and alcohol, which now makes her 100% lost to this life. [24]

Although Sherman's testimony was focused on the realm of stripping, the same factors hold true in prostitution. There is no question that drug addiction has played an enormous role in the proliferation of prostitution in the United States.

Most girls who resort to selling themselves for drug money, do so by parading their bodies along certain streets that are known for their streetwalkers. When a potential "john" pulls up to the girl in his car, both parties engage in a careful cat-and-mouse game of making their wishes known without saying anything that would get them arrested if the other person is an undercover vice officer. Once an agreement has been reached, the two drive to the girl's motel room to culminate the encounter.

Although streetwalkers have been the traditional form of prostitution over the centuries (see Genesis 38), modern-day pimps have sought out other ways to ply their trade. One of the more popular forms of prostitution to emerge in the 1980s has been the masseuse. Massage parlors, which found their roots in the Geisha clubs of Japan, became a safer way to hire a girl for sex. The john wouldn't have to be concerned with being robbed, and the chances of a masseuse being an undercover cop were minimal. Even though the cost would be a little higher, the safety factor made it more appealing to many.

Modeling agencies and escort services also became venues for hookers to offer their services. Whether in the form of cheap streetwalkers, glamorous call girls, or something in-between, prostitution continues to thrive in our highly sexualized culture.

Pornographers Take the Internet

It seems that every decade had its watershed event that furthered the level of immorality in the

United States. In the 1940s, the Kinsey Reports created credibility within the scientific and academic communities. In 1953, Hugh Hefner launched *Playboy Magazine*. The 1960s was the decade that inaugurated the Sexual Revolution as promiscuity escalated. In 1971, one successful sexual comedy film opened the doors to the adult entertainment industry. The next decade saw the proliferation of home video recorder use that enabled pornographers to mass distribute feature films into American households. Then, in 1994, a new technological advance opened the doors to the most despicable forms of smut hitherto known to the public: the Internet was created.

Almost immediately, opportunistic pornographers became involved. Within months of the Web's inception, there were 200 businesses using it to sell "erotica services," including the Playboy Empire.[25] In August 1995, a Yahoo search discovered 391 adult content sites. A study of one web browser stated that 47% of the 11,000 repeat searches were for listings with adult content.[26]

Pornographers began making big money very quickly. Seeing the enormous potential at hand, some entrepreneurs started investing resources into new technology. Seth Warshavsky, founder of Internet Entertainment Group (IEG), was the first to offer e-commerce software, allowing viewers to access adult web sites through the use of secure credit card transactions. This was enormously important because the purchase of sexual images must be quick, secure and private for it to succeed. His company also developed a new transmission technique that made it possible to view streaming video. Other companies used videoconferencing technology to deliver live strip and/or sex shows.

Online smut exploded during 1997. According to one computer magazine, in less than three years after the advent of the Internet, there were now over 10,000 adult entertainment listings.[27] A company handling credit card transactions said that in 1997, pornographic web sites were bringing in anywhere from $10,000 to $1 million per month in revenues. According to Forrester Research, analysts of the Internet industry, in 1997 adult entertainment made $137 million off the Web.[28]

From April 1997 through December 1998, the number of Internet users grew from 100 million to 150 million. IEG hit its peak in 1997-98 when they published nude photographs of radio shrink

Dr. Laura Schlessinger and offered a private pornographic video featuring popular couple Pamela Anderson and Tommy Lee. Warshavsky became dubbed the Bill Gates of the Internet porn business as his web sites alone generated annual revenues of between $50-$100 million. Just one of his sites was being visited over 7 million times per day. According to industry analysts, smut sites were now generating $1 billion a year in revenues.

By 2000, there were over 40,000 web sites with sexual content according to *U.S. News & World Report* (3/27/00). Author Brendan Koerner added, "Nielsen NetRatings report that 17.5 million surfers visited adult sites from their homes in January (2000), a 40% increase compared with four months earlier." Gross revenues were now reaching $2 billion.[29]

Corporate America Enters the Porn Business

There was a time when no corporate executive in his right mind would consider tarnishing the image of his organization by being involved with pornography. But times have changed.

Today, some of the biggest purveyors of adult entertainment are respectable behemoths listed at the top of Fortune 1000. Estimates of revenues from the pornography industry range from $10-$56 billion—staggering numbers that greedy companies want to tap into. PBS notes one aspect of this huge windfall:

> Between 1992 and 1999, according to research by Showtime Event Television, pay-per-view revenues went from $54 million to $367 million. In 1998, the adult content market earned roughly $1 *billion*, according to Forrester Research. By 2001, the total was up to $14 billion—bigger, according to some estimates, than football, baseball, and basketball combined.[30]

Just like the enormous profits of pornography did not go unnoticed by gangsters in the 1970s, neither were they missed by corporate America in the 1990s. For instance, AT&T began distributing X-rated programming via The Hot Network. Not only was AT&T Broadband making huge profits, but they didn't even have to mention any of this

in the company's annual report. Author James
Lacey explains how AT&T became involved:

> Not too many years ago, AT&T stock
> was such a safe store of value that it was
> known as the "widows and orphans"
> stock. Since telecom deregulation, AT&T
> management has appeared intent on
> destroying as much of this wealth as
> possible. After losing billions on its foray into
> the cable business, management became
> desperate to improve cash flow. This has
> caused them to adopt methods that would
> have made the widows and orphans shudder.
> Cable may have been a bad investment, but
> it did offer one road to improved profits.
>
> AT&T does not say how much money
> it makes pushing porn into subscribers'
> households, but Wall Street analysts place
> it in excess of $20 million a month...
>
> Wall Street insiders note that the
> combination of AT&T and Comcast
> will make the combined entity the largest
> purveyor of porn in the country. Cable,
> however, is not AT&T's only foray into

porn. Together with MCI WorldCom, AT&T dominates the 1-900 phone-sex market. By allowing mostly lonely men to talk dirty to women, these two firms add almost $1 billion a year to their bottom line.[31]

General Motors has also sunk its corporate teeth into the porn pie. Through its subsidiary DirecTV, GM is channeling explicit movies into millions of homes. According to the Christian Science Monitor, "General Motors' satellite-television subsidiary now sells more graphic sex films than Larry Flynt, who publishes *Hustler* magazine...Large media corporations find pornography hard to avoid because of its easy profits. The shows are cheap to make and have grown into a $10 billion-a-year industry."[32]

How many of these homes are actually viewing these sleazy movies? One industry insider said, "We know what's called a 'buy rate,' which is that for every million homes you're in, in any given month we'll know how many times someone bought a movie. Generally our buy rates were between 10-20 percent. That's four million homes every month where people were paying to view a Vivid adult movie. That's good for Vivid, and it's good for General Motors."[33]

Entertainment analyst Dennis McAlpine believes that adult movies (both home videos and pay-per-view) annually bring in between $5 billion and $10 billion.[34]

Hotel chains have also been quick to seize upon the revenues produced by pornographic movies. Nearly every major hotel company is offering adult entertainment. Lacey observes:

> Other firms, such as On Command and LodgeNet Entertainment, both listed on the Nasdaq, provide smut to 1.5 million hotel rooms. Together they make an average of $23 a month per room for a total profit of over $300 million annually. Large hotel chains such as Marriott, Hilton and Sheraton have welcomed the porn distributors. For the hoteliers it is found money. They take a substantial cut of the porn profits and there is no cost to them for providing it.
>
> Credit-card companies, such as Visa, American Express and Mastercard, have

not been shy about cutting themselves into this market. Estimates say that Internet-porn sites sell $3-4 billion worth of smut-related products annually. Over 90 percent of these transactions are made with credit cards. The logos of these credit-card firms litter Internet-porn sites, including many dedicated to scatology and bestiality. Total profits from enabling porn transactions total well over $500 million.[35]

It is almost incomprehensible that in a mere thirty years, the sex-for-sale industry has increased to the point of being one of the most profitable areas of business in the thriving economy of the United States, employing—directly or indirectly—hundreds of thousands (if not millions) of Americans. Not only that, but this industry also boasts millions of wholly devoted consumers—many of whom are underage.

CHAPTER FOUR

THE Sexploitation of YOUTH

Adults, unfortunately, are not the only ones affected by the escalation of perversity in this country. Pornography's tentacles have extended into America's youth culture as well. Children, lacking the maturity to determine their life course, are ruthlessly preyed upon by the demonic forces of perversion.

Half a century ago, America's children were just that, children—young, impressionable, innocent. Childish dreams dominated their small world. Blushing naiveté accompanied talks about the "birds and the bees." Those days, however, are long past. Today, young girls are groomed as sensual nymphets—mere objects of desire for boys polluted by a world of salacious smut.

At this very moment, a war rages over the souls of our young people. One of the major battle lines being drawn is their sexuality. If Satan conquers there, he captures, arguably, one of their strongest and unbridled drives. The phenomenon we're witnessing today is not a passing phase, nor a harmless rite of passage. Rather, it is a calculated effort to prostrate our nation's youth before the altar of sexual lust.

The Sexualization of Young Girls

An extremely disturbing trend has emerged in America as preteen girls are increasingly being presented even to adult males as sex objects. The unthinkable has now become an acceptable practice in our society. Consider the following:

Currently, there are beauty pageants showcasing the bodies of young girls—some only six years old. Many, citing the use of heavy make-up, elaborate hairdos, and even false eyelashes, believe they are trained to look seductive.

Over the years, Hollywood has produced a number of movies which portray young girls as sexual objects. At age 13, Brooke Shields played the part of a young prostitute in the 1978 movie, *Pretty Baby*. In 1972, a young Jodie Foster played a similar role in Martin Scorcese's *Taxi Driver*. A recent movie, *Hearts in Atlantis*, shows an 11-year-old girl making out with her boyfriend. Later in the film, Anthony Hopkins himself openly touches her breasts.[36]

In her book, *Soft Porn Plays Hardball*, Dr. Judith Reisman describes in great detail how *Playboy*, *Penthouse* and *Hustler* magazines have effectively—over the past forty years—promoted adult-child sex through the use of cartoons. They use cartoons, she says, "to make children adult sex objects."

Unfortunately, pornographers aren't the only promoters of this atrocity. Judith Levine, in her recently released, *Harmful to Minors: The Perils of Protecting Children from Sex*, stresses that young girls and boys should be allowed to make their own decisions regarding sex—even sex with an adult. She also endorses the Dutch law, enacted in 1990 that legalized sex between children (12 years and older) and adults providing there was mutual consent.

Without question, America is increasingly emphasizing the sexuality of its female youth. The central message to adolescent girls is: your value is found in your body, therefore, make it the focus of your expression.

Just look at the impact the music industry has had on our youth. Through its promotion of pop stars like Madonna in the '80s and present-day teen icons Britney Spears and Christina Aguilera, the music industry has systematically indoctrinated young girls to think sensually, dress seductively and act provocatively.

Britney Spears' influence on young American girls has been devastating. It's common to see "good girls" singing and dancing sensuously to her latest song, Britney's "take me" look posed on their faces, hoping the cute boy *du jour* will notice them.

Ms. Spears, who recently "French" kissed Madonna on MTV's music awards show, dismisses parental concerns about her harmful influence. "When someone tells me not to do something, I do it, that's just my rebellious nature," she said. "...they shouldn't be concerned because they should trust their kids and believe in their kids."[37]

Far from a cultural phenomenon, Britney Spears is merely a reflection of a larger movement that is changing the way preteen girls dress. Fashion designers now compete over who can produce the "sexiest" new clothes, marketing them to teens with risqué ads. The leading crusaders in this campaign to sexualize our youth are the popular retail clothing chains. One of these, Abercrombie & Fitch, was recently criticized for its line of thong underwear for little girls and a pornographic catalog distributed to kids.

Clearly, girls are being taught that, to be popular, noticed, and have more "fun," they must wear more revealing clothing. Even girls who sincerely desire modesty, find it increasingly more difficult to find clothing that is not too revealing but still get "style points" from their peers.

Teenage Promiscuity

Our present-day culture not only pressures young girls to dress provocatively, but it also encourages them to *think* sexually. Popular network TV shows such as *Friends*, *Dawson's Creek*, *Boston Public*, and others are feeding our children a steady

77

diet of "acceptable" promiscuity. Like it or not, the actors and actresses on these shows are today's youth role models. They teach our kids to associate free, unrestrained sexual expression with success, happiness, power, and "love."

Hollywood promotes this message in movies like *American Pie, Crazy/Beautiful* and others, showing older teens experiencing the "thrills" of sex with no apparent side affects. Moreover, these same movies serve up casts of young nymphets who are all too willing to supply their male Romeos with sex, albeit for a cheap twisting of their romantic arms.

Television further strengthens the message by offering a step-by-step guide on seducing women. Viewers are relentlessly bombarded with commercials featuring voluptuous women as mere sex objects. Popular sitcoms often show "Casanovas" instructing young boys in the art of manipulation. The goal, of course, is to feign sincerity and charm the girl into having sex. Recently, shows are casting adults in roles that sympathize with young boys' desires for sex and encourage their fulfillment of those desires. The AFA Journal provides one such example:

In the June 6 episode of NBC's *Will and Grace*, Jack, the shows' flamboyant homosexual, asks thirty-something Grace to accompany his 12-year-old son Elliot to his first school dance. Jack attends the dance as a chaperone, and when he discovers that the girl Elliott likes is there, he tries to encourage his son to ask her to dance. Grace objects, insisting that Elliott should learn to stay with whomever he takes on a date. Jack gets angry with Grace, insisting that the only important thing is that he wants to 'get my kid some tail.'[38]

Unfortunately, trivialization of sex on network TV is becoming the accepted norm. A recent study by the Kaiser Family Foundation found that the percentage of programs with sexual content increased from 56% in the 1997-1998 television season to 68% in the 1999-2000 season. "Every year in this country, there are three-quarters of a million teen pregnancies and 4 million cases of sexually transmitted diseases among teens," said Kaiser's Vicky Rideout. "Now, we're not blaming TV for this, but we are saying that young people watch a lot of TV. There's obviously a lot of sex on TV, so it's important to think about the messages about sex that television is communicating." [39] Increased sexual content may be affecting young people more than we think. According to the American Academy of Pediatrics Committee on Public Education:

> By the time adolescents graduate from high school, they will have spent 15,000 hours watching television, compared with 12,000 hours spent in the classroom… American media are thought to be the most sexually suggestive in the Western hemisphere. The average American adolescent will view nearly 14,000 sexual references per year, yet only 165 of these references deal with birth control, self-control, abstinence, or the risk of pregnancy or STDs. [40]

Another contributing factor in the corruption of young girls is the content in teen magazines. In a recent FoxNews.com article, Catherine Donaldson-Evans wrote the following:

They feature sexy male centerfolds, flirty innuendos and relationship advice. Women's magazines? No. They're magazines for teens.

In the most recent issue of *CosmoGIRL,* for instance, there are tips on meeting guys, as well as a sexy pin-up of 29-year-old actor Paul Walker and an interview with him: "We got him to strip down and bare everything ...about himself, naughty girl!"

According to a pair of studies released last month, 70 percent of American teens get information about sex from the media—and 20 percent have had sex before age 15.

So are mags aimed at adolescents too sexed-up—or is their approach to issues facing today's youngsters realistic?[41]

That such a question can be seriously asked today is evidence of our moral decline. Thankfully, there are those few willing to take a stand for decency. Elayne Bennett, president of Best Friends Foundation, an abstinence program for adolescent girls, complained, "Magazines are marketing sex in a big way…These magazines do not take a stand. They aren't saying sex is not really for you at this time in your life. That's where parents and teachers think they've fallen short."[42]

Unquestionably, young people in post-modern America are being taught that traditional morals are antiquated and unnecessary. A recent survey shows that 63% of teenagers believe, "waiting to have sex is a nice idea but nobody really does it."[43] These numbers are corroborated by figures released through the American Academy of Pediatrics stating "61% of all high school seniors have had sexual intercourse, about half are currently sexually active, and 21% have had 4 or more partners."[44] Additionally, the National Campaign to Prevent Teen Pregnancy has found that approximately 20% of teenagers had engaged in sex before turning 15 years old.[45]

Pornography Exposure and Usage

Perhaps the single most distressing influence on youth over the last three decades has come via the porn industry. Long before there was a World Wide Web loaded with sexual content, both

national commissions on pornography (1970 &
1986) concluded that boys age 12 to 17 are among
the largest consumers of adult material. How
much more true is it today, when most kids have
unsupervised Internet access either at home, at the
home of a friend, at school, or at the library?

"At this very moment…" barked Attorney
General John Ashcroft during a recent address,
"panderers of obscenity are amassing their
fortunes at the expense of our children's health
and innocence."[46] Lest we dismiss this as simply
political rhetoric, consider the following:

In a 1999 survey, National Public Radio
reported that 31% of children age 10 to 17
from households with computers (24% of all
kids in that age range) said that they had seen
a pornographic web site.[47] *Time* magazine, in
2000, stated the number to be even higher: 44%.
According to a recent study by Internet security
provider Symantec Corporation,[48] 47% of the
children surveyed had received pornographic
spam. A similar study of children ages 8 and 16
reported that 9 out of 10 had visited an adults-only
website.[49] Regardless of these figures' accuracy,
the frightening reality is that millions of America's

kids are being exposed (at an average age of 11![50])
to the evils of pornography.

"Finding porn on the Web is easier than
researching for a homework assignment," one
fourteen-year-old told MSNBC. "What kid can't
type in porn.com? It's constantly being blasted
at (us) from all directions." A fifteen-year-old girl
from a Christian family said, "Most of the time, I
stumble upon the porn sites. For instance, I was
looking for pictures of elephants for my aunt and
I stumbled upon pictures of women having sex
with animals, not a pretty picture."

EPILOGUE

Without a doubt, our nation has been fully immersed in a "sex is everything" mindset. The warped thinking initiated 60 years ago by Alfred Kinsey has polluted millions of minds. The sexual underground Kinsey spawned is rapidly becoming an accepted component of mainstream America.

People, of all ages and in all facets of our society, are now regularly involved in illicit sex! The bank teller you see every Friday is thoroughly entrenched in the gay lifestyle. The girl standing in line ahead of you at the store is an exotic dancer.

The guy sitting next to you in church frequents massage parlors. The little boy next door—he's addicted to Internet pornography.

It must not be overlooked that all of these people have been terribly warped by the evil thinking that both proceeds and accompanies these lifestyles. For instance, it has become increasingly clear that pornography promotes:

- Sexual addiction and promiscuity.
- Unhealthy attitudes about sexuality.
- The dehumanization of women as sex toys.
- The rape myth, that women actually want to be raped.
- Sexual relationships apart from love and commitment.
- Selfish indulgence and isolation.
- Aberrant and bizarre sex.

The Church has certainly not been exempt from the affects of this moral disaster either. Shockingly, studies and polls have shown that the percentage of Christian men regularly viewing pornography is the same as that of nonbelievers (about 20%). According to a poll conducted by *Christianity Today* in 2001, 44% of pastors acknowledged that they had visited a smut site.[51] There is every reason to believe that these percentages have grown substantially since then.

All this begs the inevitable question: How is this affecting the Body of Christ? When Jesus warned us to "beware of the leaven of hypocrisy," He was communicating to His listeners that even though a hypocrite hides his sin from those around him, it still has a detrimental effect on the lives of others. The metaphor of leaven is used to illustrate the corrupting influence of a small ingredient upon the rest of the dough. Unfortunately, in the case of the 21st Century Church, we are talking about the influence of millions of men who are outwardly presenting themselves as religious while inwardly maintaining a virtual mental library of pornographic images.

Despite the soothsayers who minimize the damage being done, pornography is a spiritual disease running rampant through the Christian community. In short, we show all the signs of suffering from a spiritual epidemic.

If it is true that one out of every five men sitting in America's pews is saturating his mind with the evil images of pornography, how does this affect the overall level of godliness in the Church? The answer is devastatingly obvious: The general urgency to live a consecrated life is now at an all-time low. Self-centered living has all but replaced true sacrificial love. A hunger for God has been supplanted by a lust for entertainment. While the Church is weathering a fierce spiritual onslaught from without, the godly character needed for this battle rots within.

I believe with all my heart in the Church Triumphant. However, if we are ever going to return to the godly living of our forefathers, we must face the blight of pornography and sexual sin in an honest and forthright manner. The greatest threat to the Church today is not so much the pornography itself as much as it is the lackadaisical attitude many Christians have toward its sinful nature. Minimizing its wickedness might alleviate some of the shame for those using it, but it will not aid in halting the epidemic. Let's recognize pornography for the evil thing it is. Perhaps then we can effectively help those contaminated by it and do more to arrest its incursion into the Christian ranks.

NOTES

1   Judith A. Reisman, PhD., *Kinsey: Crimes & Consequences*, Institute for Media Education, Inc., 1998, p.7.

2   Reisman, *Sex revolution triggers national impotence*. © 1999 WorldNetDaily.com.

3   Morris Ploscowe, 1948. "Sexual Patterns and the Law" in *Sex Habits of American Men, A Symposium on the Kinsey Reports*, Albert Deutsch, Editor, New York, Prentice Hall, pp. 133-134.

4   Reisman, *The Kinsey Reports: The Authority for "Abolishing" Legal Protections for Women and Children in the States' Criminal Codes*, RSVP America.

5   Wechsler, H. 1955. A Thoughtful Code of Substantive Law. *Journal of Criminal Law, Criminology and Police Science*, Vol. 45, pp. 524-535.

6   Jonathan Gathorne Hardy, *Sex the measure of all things*,

p. 376.

7   Leslie Renky, Kentucky Penal Code, Final Draft, November 1971. Kentucky Crime Commission, Sec. 1100.

8   SIECUS, *Guidelines for Comprehensive Sexuality Education*, the National Guidelines Task Force, 1991, p. 9.

9   International Organization of Heterosexual Rights (*www. inoohr.org/siecussexologistsviewsonpedo.htm*)Mary Calderone in a 1980 speech to Association of Planned Parenthood Physicians.

10 *ibid*, Mary Calderone on panel: *Childhood, the First Season: Nurturing Sexual Awakening discussion of masturbation, sex play, sexual abuse, nudity and body image issues.* SSSS Eastern Region Conference. April 20, 1985.

11 *ibid*, Wardell B. Pomeroy in a 1978 speech to Third International Congress of Medical Sexology in Rome.

12 *ibid*, Wardell B. Pomeroy, "A New Look at Incest," *Forum Magazine*, November 1976, pps. 84-89.

13 *ibid*, James Rainey, EdD, *Dealing with the Last Taboo*. SIECUS Report, May 1979.

14 *ibid,* Elizabeth Allgeier, SIECUS report May/July 1982, p.8.

15 Steve Gallagher, *Break Free from the Lusts of this World*, Pure Life Ministries, 2001.

16 Dr. Judith Reisman, *"Soft Porn" Plays Hardball*, Huntington House Publishers, Lafayette, LA, 1991, p. 25.

17 Hugh Hefner, *Playboy* (January 1989), p. 5.

18 Chris Colin, Brilliant Careers, Hugh Hefner (www.salon.com).

19 Dr. Judith Reisman, *ibid*, p. 25.

20 Norma McCorvey, *Norma McCorvey (Jane Roe of Roe v. Wade) and Sandra Cano (Jane Doe of Doe v. Bolton) speak out against abortion,* Women and Children First, (*www.roevwade.org*).

21 Norma McCorvey, *ibid*, World News Tonight, ABC, 8/10/95.

22 The Attorney General's Commission on Pornopraphy, Rutledge Hill Press, 1986.

23 Citizens for Community Values, www.ccv.org.

24 *ibid*.

25 M.W. Strangelove, "Internet advertising review – The Internet has hormones," Selling Sex in Cyberspace, *The Internet Business Journal*, p. 10, Jan. 1995.

26 S. Connor, "Pornography most popular subject for Internet searches," *The Independent – London*, Sept. 13, 1995.

27 *Inter@ctive Week* survey results, "X-rated sites pace online industry," *Chicago Sun Times*, 24 June 1997.

28 "Surfing for sex," *The Guardian*, May 14, 1998.

29 Much of the history of Internet porn detailed in this article comes from an article written by Donna M. Hughes, *The Internet and Sex Industries: Partners in Global Sexual Exploitation* for Technology and Society Magazine, Spring 2000.

30 Nicholas Confessore, *Porn and Politics in a Digital Age*, www.pbs.org.

31 James Laccy, *Porn Now a Staple of Big Business*, Nov. 13, 2002.

32 Laurent Belsie, *Fending off stealthy growth of porn*, www.csmonitor.com.

33 www.pbs.org/wgbh/pages/frontline/shows/porn.

34 *ibid*.

35 James Lacey, *ibid*.

36 I witnessed this myself while on a plane, although I was trying not to watch the movie.

37 Associated Press, *Britney Says She's a Role Model*, November 17, 2003.

38 OneMillionDads.com. American Family Association.

39 The Kaiser Family Foundation, *Sex on TV: Content and Context.* Quoted by Kiesewetter, John and Richelle Thompson, *TV's sex content climb, study says*, Cincinnati Enquirer online, 2/07/01.

40 American Academy of Pediatrics Committee on Public Education, *Sexuality, Contraception, and the Media*, 1/2001 http://www.aap.org/policy/re0038.html.

41 Catherine Donaldson-Evans, *Teen Mags Tackle Sex*, Fox News Network, June 5, 2003.

42 *Ibid.*

43 Julia Davis, senior program officer at the Kaiser Family Foundation, quoted by the Associated Press, *Survey: Teens feel pressured to have sex,* May 20, 2003.

44 American Academy of Pediatrics Committee on Public Education: *Sexuality, Contraception, and the Media*, January 2001.

45 The Associated Press, *Survey: Teens feel pressured to have sex.*

46 OneMillionDads.com. American Family Association.

47 *Survey Shows Widespread Enthusiasm for High Technology.* (Taken from a new poll by National Public Radio, the Kaiser Family Foundation and Harvard's Kennedy School of Government.)

48 Reuters News Agency, June 9, 2003. Symantec commissioned Applied Research, a market research firm, to conduct the study.

49 London School of Economics, January 2002, as reported by Bsafehome.com.

50 *Dallas Morning News*, DallasNews.com, October 8, 2003.

51 Christianity Today, *Leadership Journal*, December 2001.

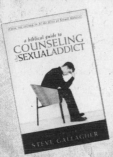

CREATE IN ME
A PURE HEART

ANSWERS FOR STRUGGLING WOMEN